Speculative Books

Glasgow

ISBN: 978-1-912917-02-0

Words: Robert Florence

All Rights Reserved

© Copyright 2018

POETRY & SWEARING: VOLUME I
by
Robert Florence

THE BOOK YOU ARE HOLDING

UP THE HILL

SAUCHIEHALL

THE DEATH-RAIN THAT FELL UPON THOSE

WITHIN THE PAGES OF THE BOOK UNWRITTEN

THE 16 AND THE 12

CATHY'S GAUN IN FOR A BIOPSY

I MET BRUCE LEE IN SHETTLESTON

AL JOLSON

ROOFER

ON THE NIGHT TERRORS

I SUFFERED AS A CHILD

20 THINGS THAT TAXI DRIVERS HAVE SAID TO ME

THE LASSIE AT UNI WITH THE FUR COAT

POEM FOR BABIES

I ONLY SEE MY DAUGHTER HALF THE TIME

YOUR DA'S GONNAE BATTER YOUR BOYFRIEND

YOUR MA SLEPT WITH A HUNNER GUYS

POEM/GLASGOW

YOU'D BE FAT AS FUCK IF JAY-Z WAS YOUR PAL

ON SEEING FRIENDS SHARING WORDS OF HATE
ON FACEBOOK
AUDREY'S DUG
THE RUMOUR OF A SHOE
JESUS CHRIST THEY KILLED THEM
ALL THE CUNTS I HATE
I WORK ON THE WALTZERS
ON FINDING THAT PESTS
HAD MADE IT INTO THE RAISED BED
THE SUBWAY
BATMAN'S AFF HIS NUT
THE FIRST TIME I DIDN'T DIE
IN THE FOREST OR THE SNOW
MY SPACESHIP WAS DOCKED AT THE ROYAL
YOUR DA
ON THE SALE OF MY PARENTS' HOME
THE ROADHOUSE
AFF YE FUCK
(from the traditional)
JUST DOWN THERE

THE BOOK YOU ARE HOLDING

hello

I am the book you are holding

hold me close to your heart

read me and when you are done with the reading

read me again from the start

read me through when you don't feel much like reading

and read me whenever you do

trust that whenever you do choose to read me

I will not be reading from you

I will not know of all the pain that's inside you

I won't be aware of your plight

I will not be watching you while you are sleeping

from my place beside you at night

I never do dream of the Palace of Pages

I don't dream of bringing you there

My cover does not rise and fall with your breathing

I don't dream of touching your hair

I don't dream at all, I am nothing

am nothing

am nothing

but paper and ink

I'm nothing

I'm nothing

I'm nothing

I'm nothing

read me and read me

don't blink

poetry:

(noun)

1. literary work in which the expression of feelings and ideas is given intensity by the use of distinctive style and rhythm;

UP THE HILL

I am living up the hill
and everything I need is here
or just down there
down by the river
that shining mirror
reflecting my life back at me

Love lives up this hill
but look
love lives down there too,
down by the river,
and everywhere

for in our home
laughter carries outside
to tumble down the lawn
across the roofs into the Clyde

my sweetheart's laughs
and the laughs she makes from me
turn out and further west
and further west
into the sea

swearing:

(noun)

1. the use of offensive language

SAUCHIEHALL

A boy is shouting loud about a coat
have you seen it, it was suede and tan
his pals are off their faces, eyes like hoops
they're queuing at the noodle bar for scran

A guy is bleeding bigtime from the face
he's striding past the taxi rank at speed
he looks like he is ready for round two
he smells like Lynx deodorant and weed

A woman wearing kneepads blows a kiss
it floats away into electric air
to settle birdlike on the art school roof
back aways before it wasn't there

The bouncer outside Sleazys takes a pen
and leaves his mark upon a pale young hand
an abstract doodle that in days to come
a school teacher will try to understand

A guy with big tattoos has gone taps aff
tomorrow he will want to disappear
tonight he treats the one he loves like shite
"*It wasnae me,*" he'll say. "*It was the gear.*"

A street is just a street is just a street
but some streets are a living artist's scrawl
upon the city, drawn by drunken hands
thus were you created, Sauchiehall

A lassie has her shoes off in the rain
her tights are laddered right up to the knee
"*Gonnae ask that cunt the fuckin' time?*"
"*It's 3am,*" I say.

The cunt is me.

Well, hello.

My name is Robert Florence (you can call me Rab, if you like, I cannae hear you so it makes no difference) and this is my poetry book.

Why a poetry book, and not – say – a big 500 page fantasy novel that gets its own movie adaptation?

Simply put – giant, franchise-building fantasy novels are too easy for a guy like me.

Easy meat, mate.

THE DEATH-RAIN THAT FELL UPON THOSE WITHIN THE PAGES OF THE BOOK UNWRITTEN

The monk squeezed the trigger-thing
on his gun-sword
a lash of crackling cold flame
licked James in half
from his balls to the parting in his hair.

One half of the romantic poet went over the table
into the fat man's lap, a quivering madness of meat
a quivering
a madness of meat.

The other half stood for a moment
a moment,
then hopped forward and slapped
down on the floor with a slippery thud.

Landing *butter side down*, you might say.

The older man fainted outright.
Thomas' gaze shifted
to the surreal sight of his friend
lying sideways on the floor
perfectly halved
like a hot scone.

He looked as if the floor had been laid around him
like the floor had been arranged around him
as if it was arranged
and that the other half of his body might be
underneath
one eye on the mice and the beetles
half-smiling in the darkness
keeping an insane secret.

Here's a secret:
You will never have the time
to do all the things
you dream of doing.

Thomas decided he would run for it.
And he would have, had his legs
responded to his mind's cries.

Wilkes was awake now. 66 years old

he had owned this pub since his father had died
that had been thirty-odd years ago.
He had seen stabbings, impromptu duels,
the clubbing to death of a rabid hound
(that had been the worst by far)
but he had never seen anything like the
ghastly scene unfolding before his waking eyes.

Here's a secret:
You may see worse things than this.

'*Oh Lord!*' Wilkes screamed.
He was not a churching man but it was an
oh lording occasion, for sure.

'*Hut kanetat den tustin Missun!*'
the monk screamed back at him.

One flash of that incredible weapon
Wilkes' face was liquid and smoke.
No mess yet seen in the small stone house
matched the sputter and spray of blood
as the old man tried to hold together

his brain
and skull
and soul
and whatever it is
we think
God gives us when we are formed from the clay.

Thomas wobbled to his feet.
He knew his horse was just outside.

If he could just get out
and into the small livery
he would pull himself onto its back

hold tight and lash it like never before.
It would carry him through the wind and rain
all night if it had to.
Its unflinching trust
would let him push it on

                and on

                              and on

until they were away from this nightmare scene.
He would take some of his own money
money saved for his education
he would make that horse
the best kept horse in all England.

But right now, he was busy watching
his own fingers stripped from his right hand,
as the monk started on him.

Here's a secret:
This monk will someday start on you.

It was the monster's intention
to leave nothing alive
in this place.

Thomas found it almost comical that
as the weapon slashed into him,
and burned parts of him away in a strange,
painlessly clean way he couldn't comprehend,
he heard a little sigh in his own throat.

A little
oh dear
kind of sigh.

Then he went the way of all things
real and unimagined.

The monk stepped over the bodies
went to the crude bar.
He tipped a mug with one of those ugly hands
looked at the liquid inside.
He dipped one finger
brought it into the darkness of the hood.
A smacking of the lips.
A taste.
He pushed the mug aside.
With his heavy boot
he flicked a severed finger across the floor.
He knew not whose finger it was.
He wasn't yet entirely sure what a finger was
or what purpose it served.
But it was ugly, and he didn't like it.
He didn't like any of these living things.
They seemed...false.
He looked at his weapon again.
It had served him well
as it always had.
It needed no reloading
and its aim was impossibly true.

He trusted it more than anything or anyone on any world.
He didn't know the weapon's name.

Only that it had been dreamed
by a ten year old boy of this world,
in the time of AD 1987.

'Hut kanetat den sunet ten kanet,' the monk said
and fired his weapon into the corpses
in honour of the young boy's
wonderful mind
and existence.

And then,
he waited.

I was born and raised in North Glesga, up in Balornock.
That's just round the corner from Barmulloch, and barely a kick in the arse away from Springburn.

From my house you used to be able to see the world famous Red Road Flats, before they were levelled, and they were quite a sight – like the monoliths out of 2001 if they were less focused on the evolution of man and a bit more into selling eckies.

And it's true to say that my bit (that's what we say in Glasgow "*Up mah bit.*") was considered a bit rough, a bit dodgy. If you were wanting to persuade people they would be safe when they visited you, you'd tell them that you were "*near Bishopbriggs*".

Bishopbriggs was the "*fancy bit*" that everybody from my area would call "*Spam Valley*" - suggesting that the dafties in Bishy spent so much money on their overpriced houses that they could only afford to eat spam.

Anyway, I could go on and on about mah bit, but I'll save that for my inevitable autobiography when things get desperate.

All you need to know is that to get to Balornock from the toon (the City Centre), you'd need to catch a bus.

And the numbers you'd be after would be
the 16 and the 12.

THE 16 AND THE 12

I used to get the 16 from the toon up to my ma's
it was like entering a fucking lion's den on wheels
change in your haun like you were grippin' a knuckleduster
steppin' onto that fuckin hing
you'd carry oan aw the courage you could bring

The 16 took me fae Queen Street up tae Wallacewell
And it went by Petershill and the Red Road Flats
And you'd hope to god you didnae end up sitting beside
a right fuckin nutter
or a passenger aff his face
you'd hink some of them had caught a bus tae space

If you were really fuckin unlucky you would have to get the 12
Which took you through Barmulloch noo anaw
So you'd fire past the Broomy, Torryburn and Quarrywood
like driving through Pompeii
On the day the volcano erupted, I mean to say

And you'd be on that fuckin' bus, heid doon, eyes to flair
As it rumbled up through Glesga tae the North
And you'd have your wits aboot ye, spider-senses on the go
Cos it could aw kick aff in a minute
some cunt could dream up a nightmare, and you'd be in it

There'd be auld guys, mad auld alkies
on their way back fae the pubs
there'd be young guys bangin windaes up the back
there'd be wummin being racist right up front
right out loud and you wouldnae say a thing
decades later, the guilt of that would sting

Jesus fuckin help you if you had to go upstairs
Like climbing helter-skelter steps to Hell
I saw a lassie giein' a blowjob to a guy who was shootin' up
saw that with these eyes
what an image for a child to analyse

Where do all these people live, I used to think to myself
Where do all these fuckin' psychos live?
Cos see, for me, I left the bus and walked into my ma's.
And then 16s and 12s didnae exist
They nightmare-wagons disappeared like mist.

Nae alkies, nae wee maddies, nae pale junkies sucking dicks
Nae roaring voices, cursing, swearing, no
My stop was at a place of peace and warmth
and love and trust
I didnae know that real life was the bus

If you're a comedy writer in Glasgow, writing a lot of dialogue for Glaswegian characters, you just love to listen to people talk. Glaswegians are great at talking. Absolute champions. And, guaranteed, if I'm to ever overhear any kind of conversation in the wild, I'm going to stop to listen.

But this isn't just a writer thing. It's a family thing. My ma was an absolute nightmare for listening in to the conversations of strangers. She would do it in the most obvious way too – she'd practically insert herself into the conversation, positioning herself within the group, with her wee face tilted up, eyes wide, smiling. She would hang off the shoulder of the conversation like a wee Glesga chimpanzee.

It was embarrassing if you were a thirteen-year-old and you were forced to stand beside her as she did it, but it was kinda sweet too. It was like she had no awareness that you couldn't just enter a conversation that didn't involve you. It was like she thought she was everybody's pal, which might have been something to do with her being a nurse. She would just stand there, inches away from people, soaking up their conversation like a wee auburn-haired sponge in American Tan tights.

So if you ever see me out on the streets, I give you fair warning – I am coming to eavesdrop on you. Just accept it. No need for us to fight about it. You'd lose in a fight, anyway. I'm fae Balornock.

One day, I overheard this one little snippet
> *"Cathy's gaun in for a biopsy."*

It was the opening bit of dialogue from a woman to her friend on a train platform in Partick. It landed even before the "Hello", and I think that speaks to the seriousness of the subject. Out of decency, I moved along, shackling that nosy bastard within me. But the stark, dark impact of it inspired a poem anyway.

I've also changed the name of the woman.
I hope her biopsy turned out okay in the end.

CATHY'S GAUN IN FOR A BIOPSY

Cathy's gaun in for a biopsy
And she's got the jaundice
I met her son, big fat boy, Derek
Met him last night at the Londis

Cathy's no well, he said, "*My mammy's no well*"
The boy looked like shite there anaw
Big fat boy, near 40, nae missus hissel
Fucked if he loses his maw

He says Cathy fainted in Asda
Up at the bit with the fish
He might no have said it, but he thinks she's got cancer
It was written aw ower his dish

Cathy's man died a long time ago
Och aye, he's away fifteen year
The man was a bastart tae Cathy, a bastart
Least that's what we aw used tae hear

Shaggin aroon with the wummin, och aye
Slappin wee Cathy aboot
You wouldnae a thought it, handsome big fella
Always done up in a suit

But he drapped deid of a stroke in the end
Naw, mibbe a heart hing a hink
And Cathy went right aff the rails efter that
A wee bit too fond of the drink

She used to come doon tae the bingo
And end up so drunk she was sick
She'd always say tae me, "*I've nae pals here, Margaret*"
She'd lay it aw oan pretty thick

You'd see her oot walkin' with Derek, her boy
Him on his crutches, her steamin
She'd say "*Aw, he'd make a fine husband, he would.*"
I used tae hink "*Cathy, you're dreamin'*"

Big fat boy, on crutches, he near cannae walk
Shoulda seen him last night at the Londis
Near greetin' - "*I hope my wee mammy's awright.*"
She won't be if she's got the jaundice

When it comes to poems that have gone down well on social media, and that is surely the marker of real meaningful success in this terrible day and age, nothing compares to my poem about the alpha and omega of modern culture - Bruce Lee and Shettleston.

After this poem, social media marketers everywhere realised that the real hot buttons for viral social media success were

> (a) a Kung-Fu icon who died 40 years ago and
>
> (b) an area of Glasgow that would see you getting your baws booted if you behaved like a wee dick.

I present this poem, intact in its original form.

I MET BRUCE LEE IN SHETTLESTON

Check oot this wee prettyboy
Let's rattle his wee jaw
I'll knock his wee shades aff his face
Skelp his dish red raw
He's looking at us
"*Ho there, wee man!*"
"*That your mammy's blouse?*"
Noo he's went aw quiet
He's like a fuckin' mouse
Haud oan. Is he vibratin'?
What's happened to his face?
Why's he kicked his shoes aff?
This guy's a mental case!
What's that fuckin' scream aboot?
Why's he in the air?
Why's my ribcage in five pieces
Aw ower the flair?
Why am I in heaven, mammy?
Why have I nae heid?
I met Bruce Lee in Shettleston
And noo I'm fuckin' deid.

Speaking of Glasgow, when I was a wee guy, well –

 – haud oan.
Here's a poem about it.

Haud oan.

Here.

AL JOLSON

When I was a wee guy
there must have been some guy
that just cut aboot doon the Barras
painting
"*AL JOLSON*"
on aw the walls.
Or maybe just this wan guy did it
wance
and the rest were copycats.
Like the copycat killers on the cop shows
on the telly
you know the wans.
Except these ones didnae kill embdy
and they had spray paint
and they were fae Glesga
and they loved Al Jolson.
The polis must have been lit at:
"*Al Jolson?*"
They must have been lit at:
"*Whit?*"
He was some singer
to be fair.
But what about the blacking up?
Did the guy writing "*AL JOLSON*" condone that?
Forgive that?

Did he even know about that?
Or is he somewhere at a dinner party
tellin' people
"*I used tae, for a laugh, paint AL JOLSON aw ower Glesga.*
It was just a bit of surrealism.
A bit of Dada."
And then somebody Googles Al Jolson for him.
Al Jolson.
Aw blacked up, singing "*Mammy*".
And the guy like that-
"*Fucksake, man.*
I was a student back then.
I'd only heard my granny listening to him.
I didnae know."
His wife like that-
"*How could you not know?*"
Everybody looking at him.

"*He was some singer,*
to be fair" the guy says.

Everybody fuckin' glarin at him.

My da was a roofer

and the smartest guy I've ever known.

My aunties would always say to me -

"Your da could have been anything he wanted to be."

He excelled academically, but like many men of his generation he left school to go to work. There was a family to provide for, and money was tight.

My da would often tell me about his own da, Johnny, who died before I was on the scene. Johnny would come home from work and then go round all the back courts, singing up at the windows. He was busking, through the back gardens of Glasgow tenement closes, gathering up any change that was flung from the windows.

So Johnny was,

in a very real sense,

a working entertainer.

My da encouraged my writing by making me read great books, and showing me great comedy. He was happy for me to be an entertainer, like his own wee da.

But my da himself?

My da was a roofer all his days.

ROOFER

My da was a roofer
as were his brothers
and mine
out at seven, hame at six
hands black with proper work

He walked across the roof of Ravenscraig
and laid sheets above abattoirs
"*That's me aff the sausages*" he'd smile
Ask about that Lennox Castle job
he'd frown and darken, silent for a while

My da lived in digs in towns I've never seen
and here's the sorest truth of all
he saw friends die
because roofers fall
and sorer still
so must we all

My da saw his brother go before him
funny Uncle John, his heart gave out
it left a hole inside my da, a leak
some of him ran through it and away
a changed man when my uncle died that day

but what remained was good and strong
he never let the parts I needed fade
his pain he always put up out of reach
my shelter was a roof supremely made

Before my da died he said to me
"*You were always a good reader*"
Six words that meant a poem, meant a book
he never wanted me up on those roofs
he'd hitched my harness to a different hook

But still I am a roofer in my blood
I love to climb
I'm never scared of heights
But aye, da, can you hear me?
Thank you, da
Writing is what gets me through the nights

As a wee guy, I suffered fierce hallucinations on a regular basis. They spiked whenever I had a fever, but also happened during normal sleep.

It was terrible stuff. You wouldn't have been able to handle it. I handled it, but you wouldnae cope.

I think those night terrors made a huge impression upon me. I think they're why I love horror films so much, why I love HP Lovecraft stuff, and why I've always felt an affinity for anybody who believes in the supernatural. They're also probably why I've never much fancied trying any hallucinogenics - been there, done that.

Anyway – this one's about those night terrors.

They were really bad. You would have died.

*ON THE NIGHT TERRORS
I SUFFERED AS A CHILD*

It comes not creeping in the night
but screaming through the door
the hinges tearing from the wood
its jaws wide in a roar
the room folds in upon itself
my bed becomes a tree
my unlit lamp a cold, dead sun
the moon, I think, is me
the bedroom floor is miles and miles
of freezing desert dust
where corpses rise like monoliths
and insects writhe in lust
somewhere on the horizon
there is light, of life and joy
but that is where the grown men live
and I am but a boy

the screaming thing is near me now
its presence is the sea
the moon shall not control this tide
this tide will pull at me
this woman or this long-haired man
with yellow-fingered hands
upon my chest and chanting
words from devastated lands
phrases heard in sunken tombs
and songs sung by the dead
whispered, wet and secret,
through my ear into my head
the child is gone but in me still
the terror of the night
the words, the songs, the deathly chill
"*Dor fel ezath gah dzite!*"

I have this mad jaw problem called "*TMJ*".

Every time I tell somebody about it, I have to go and google what TMJ actually stands for.

So I'll be back in a minute…

Right, Im back. It stands for Temporomandibular Joint Disorder, which would be a cracking name for a band, by the way. What it means is that I have a dodgy jaw that clicks and grinds just under my ears. I've pretty much learned to tune the noise of my weird jaw out, otherwise every meal would sound like I'm dining inside the drum break of In The Air Tonight.

There was a time when my TMJ was really bad, though, and sometimes my jaw would seize or become incredibly painful.

I had to get a taxi with a locked jaw one morning, and explained the situation to the driver.

"*Cannae talk, mate. Jaw's killing me.*"

He replied - "*Aw aye? Been up aw night suckin' dicks?*"

The following poem is based on 20 true stories.

20 THINGS THAT TAXI DRIVERS HAVE SAID TO ME

01- Where ye aff tae noo, shagger?

02- These wee birds are bad for my health

03- They're giein' the cunts free beds and free fridges

04- Dae ye support the Celtic yoursel?

05- My wife moans when I'm workin', she moans even mair when I'm no'

06- The cunt pulled oot this mad big machete

   I says *"Where dae ye want me to go?"*

07- This bird with big diddies was flashin' us aw at the rank

08- I was years in the army, mate I'm trained to be drivin' a tank

09- My wife disnae like me

10- My son works in Dubai

11- Are you that boy that shouts eleven?

12- Where do you think we go when we die?

13- I'm no sayin' I'm racist but I don't trust the bastarts ataw

14- See that wee photo up there? That's my wee boy and my maw.

15- The polis are at it, they're aw fuckin bad yins themsels

16- New Year is aw played oot noo, mate. You might as well just work the bells

17- I cannae go poetry, hauf of them don't even rhyme

18- The system is loaded against us we're stuck under the fuckin' cosh of the elite as it's always been and always will be, mate. We're fuckin idiots for expecting anythin' else. Independence? It's aw a fuckin' smokescreen. The cunts will carve it up for themselves as they always dae and we'll be in the fuckin' gutter, like rats.

19- Is just here alright for ye, mate?

20- My wife's scared of cats.

I went to Glasgow University to study Film & TV.

I expected that, within months, I would be dashing around Glasgow with a 16mm camera, shooting the next big arthouse film.

I thought I'd be on the front page of The Daily Record alongside the headline "*WAN CANNES DAN!*"

(To explain to readers outside Glasgow, a Wan Can Dan is a guy that gets drunk on one can of lager. And to explain to readers from up my bit, Cannes is a film festival. To explain to everybody – this was an excellent joke.)

But no. It wasn't to be.

The course was pretty much all film theory, and I ended up writing a 5000 word essay on zombie films. Disappointed, I did the only sensible thing - I skipped lectures to watch old episodes of Columbo, spent my student loan on old Funkadelic LPs and romanticised every single encounter with members of the opposite sex.

THE LASSIE AT UNI WITH THE FUR COAT

When I was at uni, studying film
back in the 1990s
there was this blonde lassie with a big fur coat
I imagine
that in the student years of every young guy
there's this lassie
this blonde vision, with perfect skin
and big old boots
and fur
clattering into the tidy tables of your life

She'd get drunk,
and in the student union, she'd arrive at your table
and knock your drinks everywhere
and she'd laugh and flick her hair
and suddenly life would be an open road
a blacktop highway
where film students
might ride with blonde girls
forever
in an open-top red Cadillac
or something equally cliché

Her lips were like Bardot's
And she twisted your insides up like a Fellini
She knew it too
You would be in a group, discussing movies

and her eyes saw only you
Her tongue would move slowly,
calculated,
across the pink flesh below her white teeth
and you would imagine
for a moment
your own tongue underneath
hers

It was fire.
It was light.
And you knew there'd be one night -
One night, when this film would premiere
This blonde dream would be yours, if you should care

And when the moment came, it wasn't night
it was day
she asked you to her flat for coffee
and she grabbed your pinkie
and pulled it to her chest
the intentions made clear
the moment was here
she was the archetypal bee-sting lipped
fur coat-wearing
film student love affair
and the story had reached
its climactic beat

sex in the afternoon

on an unmade student bed
Bob Dylan's voice vibrating through
a dusty, smoky
sunny west end room
because of course it was Bob Dylan
of course she loved him
And you could picture it in black and white
tangled naked, you and her
illuminated in projectionist's light
in that bed until night

a memory that would never fade
a memory that could never be remade

but here's the thing
it just didn't ring
true
did it?
Sure, you were a little bit smitten
but this all felt…somehow written
A blacktop highway
with you at the wheel
of some automobile
and this beautiful blonde by your side
this teenage fantasy
too cosy, too neat
a story too often told
too predictable
a first draft at best

it didn't feel like an invitation to sex
it felt something more like a test

so you said no
and she reacted with quiet shock
her role in this story shaken
on her page of the script
it said you were taken
completely
by her

you
the film student straight as fuck white guy
like a thousand others
with the privilege of that predestination
the conquest of the blonde girl
and that drive away
into a celluloid sunset

But you said no
And both of you
over the months that follow
go your own way
she becomes a part of someone else's movie
and in time you realise
maybe the movie was hers all along
it was privilege
dumb male privilege
mainstream movie privilege
that made you feel like you were the lead

in telling this story to a friend

a few years ago

he said

in his wisdom

his crystal clear wisdom

"*Do you no' wish noo that you'd just fuckin' shagged her?*"

the blonde

the car

the dream every guy is prescribed

so dull, so dull, so harmful,

so poisoned,

so male,

so crudely described

where is that car now?

where is that girl?

you don't know if she's even alive

the love of your life would be a brunette

and you still, even now, cannae drive

I have a new baby daughter, and so I spend a great deal of my life at the moment rubbing a wee tummy and wondering aloud about how soft it feels.

I also spend a great deal of time saying words that mean absolutely nothing.

My da was a big Spike Milligan fan, and we would sit together to watch all his shows.

The daftest sketches I've written, the silliest sketches I've managed to sneak into shows I've worked on, will almost certainly have a bit of Q somewhere in their DNA.

It was a short leap to a love of Spike's poetry, and particularly his nonsense poems. So, y'know – when it came time to write a poem for my new baby daughter, this was what came out the other end.

POEM FOR BABIES

Wee plaw plum

Plumfed alang the plee

Wee plaw plum

Put popples on a bee

Wee bee with bee bee popples

Aw plumfin up the sky

Wee plumfer popples on a bee

Wee popples in your eye

Wee popples flumfed your pumplepluff

And plumfled up the stair

Wee popple bee went buzz buzz buzz

and buzzed around your hair

Wee popples in the kingdom

of butterflumpleflies

Wee plumfle buzz buzz popples

pop like magic in your eyes

Wee cutie plumfy popples

for the princess and the queen

your da's been sectioned under

Mental Health Act 2015

I think that any father, or indeed any mother, who has joint custody of a child will understand where I'm coming from with this poem. It's painful indeed to come to terms with the fact that you're only seeing your child half the time. The only way I know how to deal with it is to float through it, trying not to dig into the pain of missing her. I have to just let the ache sit inside me somehow. I focus on the excitement I feel when I anticipate the days I'll be spending with her.

She's the most amazing human being, by the way. That only makes it harder.

Whenever I've performed this poem live, I've always had someone come up to me afterwards and tell me their own story of the kids they only see on certain lucky days. And there have been occasions when fathers have told me about not seeing their kids at all.

I'm lucky all in all. Lucky that she has a great mum, and that everything has turned out so well.

The thing I love about comedy is that it encourages people to let you inside. And when you're inside, you can be honest with an audience, and they can be honest with you. Then everybody's greetin. Embarrassin', intit?

NOTE: This poem was first written when my daughter was ten. She's eleven at printing, nearly twelve. Just keeping things right for her future biographers.

I ONLY SEE MY DAUGHTER HALF THE TIME

I only see my daughter
my first daughter
ten years old

I only see my daughter half the time

I want now to describe
rather simply
if I can

how it feels to see your daughter half the time

It feels like when a poem
starts to
judder
out
it

feels like when a poem
starts to tumble out of time
and it feels
like
it feels like
when a poem
fails to meet you

you can't meet it

when YOU fail

to meet the poem at each line

and the poem starts

to cru

mb

le

out of

time

It feels like when

a poem

that you're writing

isn't quite

the one

your heart

wants you to -

hey but -

No

it's fine

when you only see

your daughter half the time

it feels like when a poem doesn't

Being a father of daughters, I often sit and think about the fact that someday – some dark day in the future – I'm going to have to deal with their boyfriends. I like to pour myself a wee dram and sit up until three in the morning thinking about this. Sometimes I go out into the woods to chop some wood while I think about it, my face bright purple as I swing my axe right through some floppy haired wee dick of a tree.

This is all old-fashioned patter, of course. And it makes you reflect on the fact that the old "*da giving the daughter's choice of partner a hard time*" thing, really makes a villain out of the father.

That's where this one comes from.

YOUR DA'S GONNAE BATTER YOUR BOYFRIEND

Your da's gonnae batter your boyfriend
He's gonnae tan his jaw
He's gonnae get some hauners
fae your granny and your maw
They're gonnae boot him up and doon the street ootside your hoose
They're gonnae kick his face until his eyes and jaw come loose
They're gonnae leave him looking like a week-old pizza crunch
Then head doon tae McDonalds for a celebration lunch
And at your boyfriends funeral
Your da will come again
tae drag him oot that coffin in the graveyard in the rain

Sometimes, when you're performing comedy for a Scottish audience, you have to play some direct football.

There's no better feeling than being in a big room full of Glesga punters, hearing them hooting and hollering to some dirty jokes. You can be as philosophical and introspective as you like, but sometimes you just need to roll in with that big wheelbarrow full of wullies and fannies and get those three wee wummin in the back row roaring.

This one seems to do the trick. I like to introduce it by talking about how beautiful poetry is. I like to talk, for a little bit too long, about why poetry is important.

"Poetry is truth. It's the song of your soul. Poetry ticks along with the rhythm of your heart. And it is the first ray of light in the breaking dawn of the human experience... When people ask me "Why poetry?" I say – because poetry is beauty.

And beauty matters..

...this wan's called "Your Ma Slept With A Hunner Guys""

YOUR MA SLEPT WITH A HUNNER GUYS

Your Auntie Brenda just turned roon
and gave ye a surprise
Your Auntie Brenda says your ma
has shagged a hunner guys

You're at your cousin's weddin'
Didnae even want tae go
And noo you just got telt a thing
You didnae want to know

You didnae want to know your ma
has sucked a hunner dicks
You didnae want to know about
your maw's menage-a-six

You didnae want to hear aboot
the fella doon the co
Oh, your mammy took him places
That he didnae want to go

She took him to an orgy in the Milton
fuelled with drugs
She made that co-op checkout guy
Have anal sex with dugs

Your Auntie says your ma and
Tommy Sheridan went oot

He thought that we should smash the state
She thought that he was cute

They used tae shag for hours
cos wee Tommy couldnae cum
Your ma went hame unsatisfied
Fake tan aw ower her bum

Your ma went oot with Taggart
the original anaw
He'd say "There's been a shaggin'"
After pumpin' your wee maw

Your ma shagged Jimmy Krankie
didnae know he was a wummin
she'd shout fandabbydozie
every time your maw was cummin

Your ma shagged Marti Pellow
Back when he was a young guy
Marti wasnae that much cop
He left her Dry, Dry, Dry

Aye here's old Auntie Brenda
aff her heid on voddy
Tellin' you your ma would only
say naw to a proddy

Aye, your ma's a right good Catholic
She goes to Sunday Mass
But just to put the organist's
big organ up her arse

I lived in Glasgow for 40 years of my life.
And then I left. 40 years is plenty.
You'd be oot of jail sooner if you murdered Glesga.
It's still the greatest city in the world, though.

Here's a poem about Glasgow,
but also about poetry,
and about me,
and about continuing on.

Hopefully it'll be about you a wee bit anaw.

POEM/GLASGOW

A city at night is like a poem.
Now, before you roll your eyes, let me elaborate.
You read poetry again
and again
and again
because it's more than a rhyme
or a story.
It's a city with words as its buildings
as you go walking through that city you can see those words
--LIT UP--
glowing with fire and light
human warmth inside them
you walk by, comforted.

There will be a time when you walk in that city at night
and you wonder what lies inside those structures
so you stare a little while through the windows.

You linger
your pace slows
and it takes so
much
longer
to get home.

What a joy it is to walk in the city at night.
Passing from verse to verse

across bridges straight and squint
staring down at water dark and deep.
What a waste to hurry home and fall asleep.

And look up too.
These buildings always show you something new.

In this city,
words are sleekit, monolithic
soft, seductive,
hard, horrific.

But all are beautiful.

They speak of history and culture, floor by floor.
A hundred ghosts behind each door.

So pass by, pass by,
pass by, slowly.

Pass by chapel, pass by mosque,
pass by close and lock-up.
Pass by nightclub,

take your time in every street you walk up.

Move from road to road to thought to rhyme to joy to meaning.

Move from

broken

sen

ten

ces

to where you'll find me leaning.

I'm always here,
inside this poem at night.
This city, this life,
this poem that would roll its eyes at itself.
I walk home so slowly,
trying to break my own defences,
peering through the keyholes,
scaling fences.

"*Polis, leave me be.*
It's just the subtext ah'm intent tae see."

Maybe halfway through my years now
and still unsure of what I'm reading.
Don't make me sleep, just let me walk,
more time is what I'm needing.

A poem

A city

A life

will make you fight for its secrets.

Friend,

keep fighting.

And try, like me, to learn to love this thing you keep reciting.

I often think about what it would be like to be best pals with really rich and famous celebrities. I don't think I'd be able to handle it. When I watch shows like The Real Housewives of Beverly Hills, it looks like these people are having parties every single weekend. And these parties are always catered right up to the max, like at a gangster's wedding.

We're talking
big giant buffets
here.

Every weekend!

I'd need to be like that

"*I cannae come. I cannae stop eating aw your scran.*"

"*Just come, Rab.*"

"*Naw, I cannae. I'm – I cannae.*"

Nightmare.

YOU'D BE FAT AS FUCK IF JAY-Z WAS YOUR PAL

Imagine you were Jay-Z's pal

Up Beyonce's hoose and that

Eating Tarka Dal

Eating a big takeaway they got

Pakora by the poolside

Samosas on a boat

Eating this big ice cream that they'd make

You couldnae even eat it all

You'd gie the rest to Drake

And then head to the kitchen with Solange

She'd talk about equality

And eat a big blancmange

Then Kanye would turn up with pizza crunch

And everybody's stuffed

so Jay-Z saves it for his lunch

And then he'd say *"We need another portion"*

Cos somebody else is hungry

It's that greedy shite Frank Ocean

Then Jay would start to cry and reminisce

About a recent dinner

With a friend he'll always miss

You'd hear he shared a Shepherd's Pie with Prince

Jay had the mash on top

And Prince just tanned the mince

Imagine you were pals with big Jay-Z

You'd end up about 20 stone

If you went to his for tea

When you see somebody you like sharing something horrible on Facebook it really sends you into a bit of a crisis. Do you really know them, after all? Do you even really know yourself?

Are you friends with a Nazi?

Are you a Nazi?

I'm sure you're not a Nazi. I think people just don't think.

Here's a poem about Facebook.

ON SEEING FRIENDS SHARING WORDS OF HATE ON FACEBOOK

One spill of hate is all it takes
The measure of a spit
Shared from page to page
without much pause to think on it

The hate begins just as a sigh
sent hissing through one door
Then click by click by casual eye
The sigh becomes a roar

The roar will rise up off the page
Becoming as a storm
To lightning bolt into the world
In some new bastard form

Presidents get made this way
other mistakes too
Be sure that nowhere in this hate
Exists a trace of you

Right, stop!

Before you read any further, get yourself on Google and search for this - "*Audrey Hepburn Dog Basket.*"

See, Audrey hepburn used to cycle about with her wee dug inside her basket. And it's just such an iconic image. Beautiful lovely Audrey Hepburn, in the past, on her bike.

Back in the lovely days. Back before Prince died.

Imagine being that wee dug.

Magic.

AUDREY'S DUG

Audrey Hepburn
On a bike
With a mad wee dug
In the basket

Does that wee dug
Know how lucky it was?
When I am deid too
I will ask it.

I love Kanye West, even through all his mis-steps.

He's an unbelievably talented individual, and I'm always very suspicious of people who claim not to recognise just how talented he is.

He's a guy who is often ridiculed in the press, and there is a general sense that people want to culturally downgrade his achievements.

When I perform this poem live, people laugh. They think I'm not being serious.

BUT THE JOKE IS ON THEM.

THE RUMOUR OF A SHOE

The sea roars.
Kanye West designs a shoe.

And while it may not be the Mona Lisa
It may not be David, or John The Baptist
it is almost
it is an expression of the artist's impulse
it is the pulsing heart of humanity

It is the burning heat of humanity
It is our tiny explosion
A desperate plea from humanity to an unthinking
unblinking universe
Kanye West.
Do you see him?
Kanye.
Kanye West.
"*Here is my shoe,*" he pleads, into the darkness.

Should you laugh, it exposes you
Because there is no foolishness in this act
No vanity in this act
No ego in this act
This is humanity.

Understand this:

Kanye West created one of the greatest albums ever recorded
A monolithic human achievement
but he rests not

Kanye West rests not
because he hears the sea
and despite knowing it is all for nothing
he swims to meet it

He clothes a shoulder
this great man.
He creates a photographic art book
this great man.
He makes a film
this great man.
He is creative director for a porn industry awards ceremony
this great man.
He sets out the blueprint for a shoe
this great man.
This human being.

Mock Kanye West
but the sea will not.
Reality is not printed in ink.
Our story is not written by those
who view passion as weakness
or belief as arrogance
But written by the roaring tide of the sea

as it swallows all things

leaving nothing but the rumour of a spark.

There comes a point in your life when death comes knocking for the people you love.

And it's a *shock*.

Even though you know that it happens, when it actually happens you're like that: "It's actually happening?"

And it is. It's actually happening.

Here's a poem.

JESUS CHRIST THEY KILLED THEM

Jesus Christ, they killed them
They killed David Bowie
They took David Bowie and they took him and they
put a disease inside him and he died
Now David Bowie doesn't exist
He can't think, feel, or create
He can't create anything new to give to us
because the bastards fucking killed him.
They killed him.
Then they came for Prince
They killed Prince
They came to Paisley Park
they put a pain in his hips
they put time inside him
they put age into him
they made him older than he was
they made him old
and then they put a need inside him
a need he couldn't control
and the fuckers killed him
They killed him
And now there is no Prince
They killed my ma and they killed my da
they put hallucinations into my ma's heid
and they made her into a shadow of what she used to be
and they took her away
bit by bit

they dismantled her

and they took her outside and they killed her

and my da --

they're not so creative these bastards

they put the same disease that killed David Bowie

inside my da's stomach

and inside his throat

and he couldnae eat

and he had pain inside

they made him weaker than I'd ever seen him

than anybody had ever seen him

even though they didnae break him

they couldnae break him

They killed him

they fucking killed my da

that's what the bastards did

And listen

listen

Now they're coming for us.

That's me in a horrible mood now, after that poem.
What an absolute downer.

So while I'm in a horrible mood, let me exaggerate my own personality for comedic effect and tell you about all the cunts I hate.

ALL THE CUNTS I HATE

Let me tell you all about the cunts I really hate
I've made a list of them inside this verse
Here are all the people that I'd like to call *"the late"*
Here's the cunts who should be in a hearse

See the guys in Finnieston who wear wee skinny jeans
talk about their favourite David Lynch
live inside a studio and blog about french cheese
I'd stab they cunts right ootside Ox and Finch

See these pricks that call themselves photographers for hire
to sleaze on lassies working on their folio
I'd take a fuckin baseball bat, rattle aff their knees
and leave them walkin like they once had polio

see that cunt in Oran Mor who plays the violin
despite naebody asking for a tune
I'd boot him in the baws so hard his manky wee moustache
would enter fuckin' orbit roon the moon

Anybody self-described as any kind of influencer
would feel the toe end of my boot anaw
Instagrammers, youtube pricks and fannies affy Twitter
I'd kill them and their viewers and their maw

Anybody who describes their own life as a brand
and measures popularity by clicks
I'd boot them in the fanny if a wummin, nice and simple,
and the guys would all get branded on their dicks

Drug Dealers I'd trap inside a flat in Broomfield Road
And shoot their fuckin' pitbulls full of drugs
Instead of systematically fucking up our weans
These cunts can all get fucked up by some dugs

Similarly, predatory cunts who invite women
into cubicles to partake in some powder
I'd meet them in that cubicle with steel-toed boots prepared
and hoof their testicles into baws chowder

Oh, and see that guy who did that fuckin Burnistoun show shite?
What a fuckin' way to make a livin'
I mean the big tall skinny wan, the other one's awright
I'd send that lanky bastart aff tae heaven*

---

*I actually love him. This is just what we call, in the game, a bam-up.

This poem is about the worst job I ever had.

And I only had it for two weeks. What am I even moaning about?

Poets are the worst.

I WORK ON THE WALTZERS

My name's Barry Joe McGhee
I used to work on the Waltzers
Purely to bam up this poet I knew
Cause nothing rhymes with the Waltzers

I wore a sweet wee denim jaicket
Fired intae aw the birds
They spun roon so quick, I'd have to seduce them
In very few actual words

I'd shout in their ear, "*Awright Doll?!*"
then I'd shout "*Fancy a winch*".
then they'd shout "*How big's your wullie?!*"
And then I'd shout "*8 or 9 inch!*"

I'd get aw the lassies a hotdog
Cause I get all my hotdogs for free
Then we would go on the Twister
The lassies would sit on my knee

That's not a safe way to sit there
When the Twister gets up to top speed
So quite a few of my wee girlfriends
Would end up with a severed heid

But Betty who worked on the ghost train
Was a spooky wee psychic anaw
So when lassies got decapitated
She'd pull oot her wee crystal baw

She'd contact Aleister Crowley
This mad auld cunt who lives in hell
She'd say "Can you fix these wee lassies?"
And he'd say "I'll fix you as well."

Then a ghost would appear from the shadows
Shag Betty hard fae behind
And Aleister Crowley's mad auld voice
would start to speak in my mind

He'd say "*My name is Aleister Crowley
A Satanist true and true.
But one of my greatest regrets, my young friend,
is I never did taste Irn-Bru.*"

So I'd go and get Ally some ginger
While Betty and him did a spell
By the time I got back to the ghost train
There'd be this despicable smell

The darkness would be full of creatures
prancing and preening with glee
Crowley had reattached my wee bird's heid
but reattached it to his knee

He's like that "*Ooh, do you want to get married!*"
He's like that "*Ooh, can I be your wife.*"
I'm just like that "*Fucksake, mate, get a grip*
Never seen such a prick aw my life."

Aye, I used to work on the Waltzers
With satanists, shaggers, oh my
But now I'm employed in a place even worse
a call centre, working for Sky.

I never really paid any attention to plants or flowers until I met the woman I love. She took me walks to places, and told me about all the berries and leaves that I could eat.

It turns out that there is free food.
Everywhere.

I love to watch her making these beautiful things grow.

ON FINDING THAT PESTS HAD MADE IT INTO THE RAISED BED

Someone is eating the crops.
The leaves of the babies you planted
in our garden
are riddled with holes.
Someone has stolen into the bed
made a feast of your care.
I will find them.
I will craft a spear
From bramble-rod and greenhouse-glass
and set off into the world.
I will track them
by the scent of their greed.
The stench of broccoli will be on their breath
and when they least expect it
I will be there.
I will speak once
"This is for she who planted flowers in my heart."
I will drive my spear deep
Into that thief.
Should anyone dare to say
"What vengeance! It was only a leaf!"
I will drag them back to our garden
you and I will sow seeds
Little seeds, of all those wonders you taught me,
Inside their hollow chest.

Glasgow's subway trains are beautiful.
I like to ride them for fun.

They're like wee pretend versions of real tube systems in other cities. They're orange. People always sit on them with wee daft smiles, as if to say:

"*Wheeee! This is fun.*
And daft.
Don't look at me.
Wheeeeee!"

THE SUBWAY

Everybody on the subway
Is younger than me.
Jeans ripped at knees,
ankles bare in little white sannies.
Coy looks to the ceiling
To the adverts
dancing around my eyeline.
Jaws tilted high
profiles perfected.
It is all performance.
A boy attempts to age himself
with glasses and a beard.
With soft white hands
He grips a hardback
small-print
wide-load book.

It's in immaculate condition.
His look is severe
but only the young are so serious.
Still, my heart flings him flowers.
Bravo!
Everybody on the subway
is younger than me.
Except one old man in a too-small hat
that reads "*Borussia Dortmund*".
Our eyes meet.
I tilt my jaw just so
to read about this interesting,
very interesting
so interesting
Italian restaurant.
The carriage rattles like applause.

By this point in this poetry collection, you're probably thinking "*Where is the Batman poem?*"

It's frustrating that a Batman poem is expected of every poet. It's unhealthy for the form and I don't understand what readers gain from it either.

Surely everything worthwhile there is to say about Batman was already said by Sylvia Plath? Am I expected to compete?

Fine. Here it is.

BATMAN'S AFF HIS NUT

Batman's aff his nut
Have you seen the way he cuts aboot
Dressed up as a mad fuckin bat
Batterin guys
I was lit at:
"*Mate, I'm worried aboot ye*
I know your ma and da died
But everybody's ma and da dies
We're no aw runnin aboot
Hookin muggers and
Kickin psychopaths in the baws."
That was when Batman went
"*Aye, but do ye ever feel like it?*
Do you ever look at the world and feel like it?
Like having a big mad base under your hoose?
Do you ever feel like drivin a big mad motor
that turns intae a tank?
Leatherin fuck oot of guys aw night?
Scarin the fuckin shite oot of them?"
And that was when I was lit at:
"Aye. Fuck it. Ah dae."
That's the Secret Origin of Robin
and everybody else.

Back to death, now.

Sorry, did I just remind you about death there?

Clear your mind. Just think happy thoughts. Think about how delicious the first plums of September are, when you've chilled them long enough in the fridge. Think about eating a big ice cream cone on a pier with your family on a sunny day. Think about your big daft dug, or cat, jumping up and licking your face or something. Or a fucking hamster, if they have tongues.

Just don't think about

DEATH

THE FIRST TIME I DIDN'T DIE

The first time I didn't die was when I was born.
The second time came moments later.
The third time I didn't die was next and I liked it
The fourth time, if anything, was greater.
The fifth, sixth and seventh time passed in a blur
The hundredth time came the same day
I think when the last time does come I will sigh:
"*Well, that's it then. That's me away.*"

One night, I sat down to explain to my tiny daughter that her Granda was dead.

Instead, she explained it to me.

IN THE FOREST OR THE SNOW

When my father died
My daughter said "*Oh no.*
We cannot find my granda in the forest
or the snow."

Just a child
how did she find the perfect way
to frame the picture of a father
fairytaled away?

I am less wise.
I foolishly awake
each morning
to pull on my winter boots
and head out into the trees.

My calls ring out to silence.
It still brings me to my knees.

The snow will fall, the trees will grow,
I will vanish too.
My darling, do not search for us,
Our tracks lead home to you.

My ma's decline was absolutely shattering.

I'd always been her baby. People would say she thought the sun shone out of my arse. And it was true. The bit about her thinking it, I mean. It didn't actually shine out of my arse.
It's a Scottish arse.
The sun doesn't make a habit of shining anywhere in Scotland.

My ma was in Glasgow's Royal Infirmary, and she was hallucinating all day, every day. We guessed that it was a combination of the onset of dementia, a cocktail of medications and maybe dehydration – hey, listen - we never really got a definitive answer to
why
it was happening.

Someone at the time suggested that it was Dementia with Lewy Bodies. It certainly seemed to fit – she commonly thought that objects were people. A cushion would suddenly become a
person and she would have an extended conversation with it.

It almost sounds funny when you write it down, but the reality of it was a living nightmare.

I became a true villain in my ma's eyes during that period.

She thought that I was laying waste to the hospital ward. She believed that I travelled in a spaceship. She was convinced that I was having multiple affairs with people from her past. I had become a total disappointment to her. It was a devastating, surreal experience – like being kicked into a David Cronenberg film overnight.

Real or not, nothing breaks you down
like your mother telling you that

in the end

you've failed her.

MY SPACESHIP WAS DOCKED AT THE ROYAL

Did I ever tell you about that Christmas when I landed my spaceship
at the Royal Infirmary?
I landed it out the back, on the spare ground, where my ma could see
it
from her hospital window
All night long.
That Christmas, I really hated Christmas trees.
Despite loving Christmas all my life,
I fucking hated them that year.
I would get out of my spaceship and come up the stairs
into my ma's hospital ward,
and I'd wreck the hospital's tree.
I'd pull aff all the decorations and fling them aboot
I'd run and jump into it, screaming.
Screaming like somebody who was losing their heid.
And my ma would say -
"*Robert, get out of that tree.*
You're showing me up."
But I'd just keep doing it, night after night,
Like I didnae care for my ma's feelings at aw.
Did I tell ye about all the wee weans I would sit with?
Wee weans that would crawl out from under my ma's bed
staun behind her curtains
lie face doon on the flair, totally still, like corpses.
I'd chat away to them, with a kind voice
a terrified expression on my face.
And I'd feel, every minute of it

like escaping in my spaceship, to anywhere else
back in time, maybe
to when my da was alive, and my ma was at hame
the Christmas tree was in the corner of the living room
naebody would attack it.
There would be nae wee weans underneath the carpet
or peeking out from behind every door.
There'd be one wee wean, me. A real wee wean.
And my ma's eyes would light up as I opened my presents.
And she wasnae at aw disappointed in the person I'd become.
Naw. I was there in The Royal and my spaceship was docked
I was having an affair with a wummin my ma knew fifty year ago
Shagging hauf the nurses
Living in a hoose with some lassie
who looked a bit like this chair in the ward
that my ma said was wearing a big lace dress.
A chair with a dress on
that I was shagging or cheating on
when I wasnae away exploring space
or destroying Christmas Trees.
My ma said to me

"*I cannae believe you'd dae this tae me.*
You used to be such a good boy."
I wanted to run away.
But my spaceship was docked at The Royal
And it's probably still there the day.

I want to thank you for reading this wee book.
Thanks for taking time out of your busy day to read my poetry.
It's a genuine kindness or daftness.

And if you also bought the book? That's even more impressive. Cheers pal.

Did somebody buy you the book? That's not quite as good.
But thanks for reading it anyway.

Are you just flicking through the book somewhere, and haven't decided whether or not to buy it yet? Are you a burglar that's broken into somebody's hoose and you're just looking for money hidden inside this book? Have you bought this book purely to look intelligent while reading it in public? That won't work.

Who are you?

Whoever you are, I've spoken a lot about my da in this collection, so I think it's time now to lighten the mood and lower the tone and talk a wee bit about yours.

YOUR DA

Your da's the best, you know he is
He's better than The Pope
He's better than The Queen anaw
Your da just wullnae stop

When stuff goes wrang inside the hoose
Your da gies you the blame
But when you really balls it up
He loves you aw the same

Your da pays for your wedding
Despite the fact he's skint
Your da supports your choice of wife
Despite that she's a bint

Or if you are a lassie
And you're marrying a guy
Your da supports your choice of man
Despite that he's a pie

Your da shares kisses with your maw
Despite her bad B.O.
when she plans IKEA trips
Your da agrees to go

If you should get intae a fight
Your da will be your hauner
Your da still has some life in him
Even though he's lost his stauner

Your da pays for your holiday
To Malia. That's cute.
When you end up in the jail
Your da will bail you oot

So gie your da a kiss today
And if you think that's silly
Remember that you came from
deep inside your auld da's willie

Aye gie your da a phone the day
And if you cannae talk
Remember that you're here
because your mammy rode his cock

Aye, gie your da a hug the day
And if you think that's daft
Remember you came fae his dick
Back when it wasnae saft

I never thought the day would come when my ma and da's home, a Swedish timber house sitting all jaunty and squinty by a Balornock dual carriageway, would be sold to another family. I always thought we'd keep it.

My ma, with her parents and brothers and sisters, were the first people to live in it - the first people ever to set foot in it after it was built way back in the 50s.

The house was full of our memories, and it was unimaginable that anyone else could ever live there. It was ours - my ma's, my da's, mine, my lovely brother, my lovely sisters - ours.

But life comes at you fast, as the kids say these days when they're not reading excellent poetry books.

My ma and da ended up - as many people do in the current climate - deid. And deid can make you rethink a lot of things in your life. The house was sitting there, nobody wanted to live in it, and so it had to go.

But it was desperately sad. It felt like another death in the family, to me. This wee wooden box that used to be full of so much life was at peace.

We had all exited the body. It wasn't the Florence family home any more.

When I think about my ma and da today, I like to picture them standing at the front door of the house, waving me off. Whenever I visited, they would stand there together at the door until I was out of sight. And the road away from the house was a pretty long one! You'd be turning back and waving for ages.

But there they'd stand,
and there they still stand,
there,
in my memory and heart.

ON THE SALE OF MY PARENTS' HOME

the Red Road Flats came
down you see
and with them came the sky
long seen from my da's shoulders
that's it by

the shows are gone from sinking ground
the ski jump, twist, the shy
my tiny hand on PAC-MAN's stick
white knuckles
that's them by

the candy floss my ma brings in from work
all sweet pink dye
my mammy in the morning
even sweeter
that's it by

my sisters and my brother
all that noise
and all nearby
the house was full of music, all that music
that's it by

that day me and my da planted a tree
in late july
in hope, not expectation
but it grew and grew
it's by

the band formed by my daughter
tambourine against my thigh
my ma on trumpet
da on castanets
Shh. That's it by.

the dug
and my wee granda
half-remembered, half a lie
no context now, no picture frame, no nothing
that's them by

Star Wars men are buried in the garden
so am I
the flats, the sky
my ma, my da,
the music
that's it by

This is my love poem. No, wait, don't turn the page.

Seriously, though – I'm in love with an unbelievable woman and I cannae believe my luck. And this is why poetry was invented, right? I don't think this one really needs much of an introduction. It's all in here, my favourite poem in this collection.

I love performing this one live, because I like to see all the women in the audience get really annoyed that their fellas have never written a poem for them. Makes me feel like a pure good guy.

Which, if you haven't worked it out by this point, I am.

THE ROADHOUSE

I'm waiting at the roadhouse in the rain
my police hat is low
in my right hand an umbrella
that is mainly just for show
Let me get wet, I need to feel it
there's something here so real I must reveal it

There's neon flashing red outside the bar
and the sound of song
I feel excitement, passion, joy, I know this can't be wrong
and so I wait
a car will drop you off in time I know
this is the kind of place that you would go

From the trailer park I hear a lonesome howl
a dog awakes
I feel inside my pocket for a pen
but just for comfort
that is when
you arrive, spilling from the cabin of a truck
I put this down to destiny, not luck

To see this was worth waiting every night
your face illuminated by the light

I'm waiting at the airlock in the hull
my visor low

in my right hand there's a weapon
but it's mainly just for show
I wait in silence
I'm an exploratory crew member
on a ship that fell to violence

Our captain's floating dead outside the bay
The life support is failing
There's no kind of response
from the commanders that I'm hailing
I don't need them
My hand is on the airlock override
If you should somehow reach this door
I'll pull you straight inside

The ship itself's in orbit round Europa
Shields are critical
Why we came here, I don't know, the motive was political
still I wait
the last surviving member of my crew
My mission here is just to be with you

And then I see a form outside the door
its hand on glass
Europa – haunted ghostly moon – it makes its final pass
oh, is it you?
I depressurise the airlock with great care
Darling, if it's you I don't need air

Europa makes a mockery of night
your face illuminated by the light

I'm somewhere in a jungle in Peru
And I am lost
I should have brought more water, now I realise, to my cost
still I plough on
I hear your sweet voice calling somewhere deep
I'll find you, will not falter, will not sleep

I'm trapped inside a building that's on fire
And I'm afraid
We all need to evacuate, that's what the message said
But I climb up
I know you must be in here, near the roof
I won't survive without you, that's the truth

Europa, ghostly moon, is such a sight
your face illuminated by the light

I'm lying here in bed inside our home
the sun is rising
It's the manner of our being here that's really so surprising
lucky me
I would have lived a million tales for this
Lived a million lives to find your kiss

Our baby lies between us, on your right
Her face illuminated by your light

swearing:

(noun)

1.the use of offensive language

AFF YE FUCK
(from the traditional)

Aff ye fuck noo,

aff ye fuck,

aff ye fuckin gan.

Aff ye fuck noo,

aff ye fuck,

fair lassie,

bonnie man.

Aff ye fuck,

into the glen,

and climb a fuckin' tree.

Aff ye fuck,

and fuck yersel

the fuck awa' fae me.

poetry:

(noun)

2. literary work in which the expression of feelings and ideas is given intensity by the use of distinctive style and rhythm;

JUST DOWN THERE

a sailor, old and cold,
his final night

stills his sails
of shining deathbed white

across the sea, he hears a sound
of laughter, from the hill

I know he lived there, long ago
I know he lives there still

SPECULATIVE   BOOKS